THE FLU and YOU

BY GERI RODDA, R.N.
ILLUSTRATED BY JIM RODDA

Copyright © 2006 by Geraldine L. Rodda
All rights reserved
Published by Pumpkin Hill Productions, LLC
Printed in the United States of America
Belaire Printing Co.
College Point, New York
Library of Congress Control # 2007920512
Summary: Basic instruction on the spread of influenza virus,
including preventive strategies and healthy habits to avoid illness.
ISBN-13: 978-0-9793602-2-0
ISBN-10: 0-9793602-2-6

Dedications...

To Phoebe, Leo, and Lyric

For Marion, Don and the purple gang.

Special thanks to...

Carolyn B Bridges, M.D., Laura Nicole Richardson, M.A. and Jennifer Morcone at the Centers for Disease Control and Prevention (CDC)
Michael Crespan, M.P.H.
George Barth, M.D.
Debbye Rosen, B.S.N., M.S.
Donna McCarthy Culbert, M.P.H.
The New Milford Visiting Nurse Association

And to my husband, family and friends who offered enthusiasm, support and love.

So learn about germs and what you can do,
to prevent coming down with a case of the flu.

A person who is sick with the germs that cause flu, can spread them by coughing or sneezing on you.

You can also catch germs so small they're unseen, from lots of those things that appear to be clean.

Germs hang out on doorknobs, keyboards and more.
Your busy hands pick up germs by the score.

Touching your mouth, nose or eyes through the day, can give nasty germs a warm, moist place to stay.

They can grow in great numbers in less than a week, making you ill, so your bed you will seek.

Sore throat and headache are things you may feel,
A cough, aches and pains may be part of the deal.
The fever is high and may last several days,
Feeling real tired is also a phase.
Your parent might give the doctor a ring.
Medicine is sometimes just the right thing.

**Drink lots of fluids and don't overdo.
It takes some time to recover from flu.**

If you are sick, staying home would be best.
Going to school would spread flu to the rest.

Crowded spaces are favorite places to pass along the flu.
Don't have a party or play date when ill.
It's not the thing to do.

A shot for most will do the trick.
It's worth the tiny needle stick.
For some the nasal spray works fine.
(If you're two to forty-nine.)
Vaccines protect not only you,
but all your friends and family too.

If out of tissues, try this quick trick.
It may prevent others from getting real sick.
Cover your cough and sneeze into your arm,
germs won't be sprayed, it works like a charm.

Wash your hands often during the day,
after the bathroom and after you play.
Do wash your hands if they look dirty with grime,
after blowing your nose, wash them one more time.
Use soap and warm water and scrub fingers too,
to the germs down the drain you'll say "toodaloo!"

Washing takes twenty seconds or more.
Try singing a song while doing this chore.
Now dry your hands and finish the feat,
your hands are now clean and you're ready to eat.
If your hands are dirty and there is no sink,
alcohol hand gel cleans in a wink.

Keeping things clean is not just for looks.
Germs can live on toys, tables and books.

Step one will wash many
flu germs away.
Step two disinfects,
killing germs which might stay.

Although not proven to protect you from flu,
these healthy habits are important for you.
Let's talk about eating, there is so much to tell.
If you choose healthy food, it will help keep you well.

Fresh fruits and veggies taste great I must say,
count all the colors you eat every day.
Bright pink and orange, green, yellow and black,
can make for you a most wonderful snack.

For other facts that are good to know,
choosemyplate.gov. It's the place to go.
Check out the plate and you will see,
what healthy foods are meant to be.

Exercise is meant to help you grow strong.
It's something to do all the year long.
Fresh air, sunshine or a cool cloudy day.
Put on your sneakers. Go outside to play.

Whether running or jumping,
your heart loves the thumping,
your lungs, they fill with air.
Your muscles are flexing, reaching and stretching,
this shows your body you care.

Don't forget about sleeping and rest.
It's needed so you can perform at your best.

So be prepared and don't be scared.
You now know what to do.
Turn the page and learn some more
on how to tackle flu.

FLU FACTS

What is influenza?

Influenza is commonly called "the flu." It is caused by influenza virus, which infects the nose, throat and lungs. Unlike many other viruses that cause infections like the common cold, the flu can cause you to become very ill. (Children are two to three times more likely than adults to get sick with the flu, and children frequently spread the virus to others.)

How does the flu spread?

The main way that flu spreads is when flu germs from a cough or sneeze of an infected person are propelled through the air and land on the mouth, nose or eyes of people nearby.

Touching something with influenza virus on it then touching the mouth, nose or eyes may sometimes infect people. The flu virus can live on objects like keyboards, telephones and doorknobs for many hours.

What are the symptoms of the flu?

Influenza usually starts suddenly and may include the following symptoms.
Fever (usually high) headache, extreme tiredness, dry cough, sore throat, runny or stuffy nose, body aches. (Diarrhea and vomiting is more common among children.)

These symptoms are referred to as "flu-like symptoms." A lot of different illnesses, including the common cold, can have similar symptoms.

How soon will I get sick if I am exposed to the flu?

The time from when a person is exposed to flu virus to when symptoms begin is about 1-4 days.

How can you tell if you have the flu?

Visit your doctor or other healthcare professional for an accurate diagnosis. There are tests that can determine if you have the flu if you are tested within the first few days of the illness.

How long is a person with flu contagious?

Most healthy adults may be able to infect others from one day before becoming sick to five days after they first start having symptoms. Young children and people with weakened immune systems may be contagious for longer than a week.

What can you do to protect yourself against the flu?

The single best way to prevent the flu is to get a vaccination each fall. The Centers for Disease Control and Prevention now recommend an annual flu vaccination for all children six months through eighteen years old.
If possible, avoid close contact with people who are sick.
Wash hands often to protect yourself from germs.
Avoid touching your eyes, nose or mouth.
Clean and disinfect commonly used surfaces.
Antiviral medications can be effective for prevention and treatment of the flu. These are prescription medications, and a doctor must be consulted before they are used.

What are some healthy habits that will aid in preventing the spread of flu?

When you are sick keep your distance from others to protect them from getting sick also.
Stay home from work, school and errands when you are sick with the flu.
Cover your mouth and nose with a tissue when coughing or sneezing.

When is flu season in the United States?

Flu season can begin as early as October and last as late as June.

Sources: Centers for Disease Control (CDC)

Important disclaimer:
The information in *The Flu and You* is for educational purposes only and should not be considered to be medical advice. It is not meant to replace consultation with your physician.

Also by Geri Rodda:

UNWANTED

INFLUENZA